IRISH TRADITIONAL CARD READING

THE COMPLETE GUIDE

Sinead Nic Cumhaill

Note for Librarians: a cataloguing record for this book that includes Dewey Decimal Classification and US Library of Congress numbers is available from the Library and Archives of Canada. The complete cataloguing record can be obtained from their online database at:
www.collectionscanada.ca/amicus/index-e.html
ISBN 1-4120-3371-3

TRAFFORD

This book was published *on-demand* in cooperation with Trafford Publishing. On-demand publishing is a unique process and service of making a book available for retail sale to the public taking advantage of on-demand manufacturing and Internet marketing. On-demand publishing includes promotions, retail sales, manufacturing, order fulfilment, accounting and collecting royalties on behalf of the author.

Offices in Canada, USA, UK, Ireland, and Spain
book sales for North America and international:
Trafford Publishing, 6E–2333 Government St.
Victoria, BC V8T 4P4 CANADA
phone 250 383 6864   toll-free 1 888 232 4444
fax 250 383 6804   email to orders@trafford.com
book sales in Europe:
Trafford Publishing (UK) Ltd., Enterprise House, Wistaston Road Business Centre
Crewe, Cheshire CW2 7RP UNITED KINGDOM
phone 01270 251 396   local rate 0845 230 9601
facsimile 01270 254 983   orders.uk@trafford.com
order online at:
www.trafford.com/robots/04-1198.html

10   9   8   7   6   5   4   3

ABOUT THE AUTHOR

Sinead Nic Cumhaill was born in 1971 and is a native of the Cooley Peninsula, a town land in Co. Louth, Ireland. She has travelled the country doing card parties and has compiled all her knowledge together to write this book. This is the first book she wrote and is currently writing her second. She has a PHD in Clinical Hypnotherapy and hopes to one day write a book on this subject also.

Dedicated to my daughter Megan

Table of Contents

Preface

Mum always, weekly, got her Woman's Way and Woman's Weekly. While she couldn't wait to read their stories, I couldn't wait to read my horoscopes, it always intrigued me.

Then, as I got older and went to college, playing poker in the canteen was a usual occurrence daily during free time. One day a girl that was in my class started to tell her meanings of the cards as she casually read her own. As I observed her, it was like I already knew what she was going to say, which to me was scary.

As the years went by, I started to get feelings, hunches that certain things would happen and they actually did. I began to know if someone belonging to me was in trouble, and so, so many times I was right.

Then I spoke to my Granny Joe regarding all this and it ended up that she secretly knew how to read cards. She told me not many people could do it and that you could surly do it if you have the feel for it. She showed me some of her meanings but as she said the meanings cannot tell you the full story, it's how you feel when reading that shows you the story.

Later that year, I befriended a girl whom, unknown to me could read cards. We sat down one night and compared meanings. This excitement and knowledge started me actually reading cards.

As a result, I would like to share my experience and feeling about the cards with as many people as possible and hence, this book is written.

Always remember the more knowledge you put out to the Universe, the more you will receive.

Introduction

The knowledge of what lies ahead has always been sought even from the past ages to the present day. It helped people prepare for what was coming let it be from Mother Nature or of other sources. In today's society, we have radar, weather forecasts and satellites to show us if danger is coming, but because these technologies were not available in olden days, people tended to turn to different methods of future telling so that they could prepare themselves for whatever was coming. But even with all our technologies in today's society, our lives are still so very much unpredictable and uncertain. Because we live in such a fast pace, we need to know if our relationships will work, our jobs secure, our life will be long etc. Even today the mystic unknown future is so very intriguing to everybody.

Where Did Cards Originate?

There are so many answers and opinions to this question, that every book that is written has its own version.

Personally, I believe they came from Spain in the 1500 century. In those days, Kings needed to know would they win their battles, were their subjects loyal to them, and were their partners in marriage also loyal to them.

The Church, then, denounced card reading, it was thought to be the work of the devil. This had no effect on their popularity. As cards spread through Europe, different regions made their own changes to their decks, regarding the suits and how many picture cards there were in a deck. Every deck has two jokers, and each reader has its own interpretation of what they mean. Some readers believe that they're their as extra cards, some say burn them as they think they're unlucky and others believe they are equivalent to the Joker/Fool card in the Tarot deck.

What a card reader needs to know about reading

Card reading is not only about knowing what each card means and reading it, it's about feeling the cards. When a client is shuffling their cards, they are actually putting their energy into the cards, they are in charge of what is in the cards. The reader then just simply sees the cards and tunes into the feeling. I know when I read cards, even though they're on front of me, I find that my gaze is slightly out of focus and I pick up on the feeling. It is this feeling that paints the true picture. Some clients who watch me while I would read have said that it seems to them that something tells me to say what I say and actually that is what it feels like. Sometimes when you're in tune you say things that are not visible there in the cards and you wonder where you got it from, and what's more intriguing is that it usually is right. I would always tell a client that before getting cards read that they are not to think intensely about any one thing, it can mislead their cards. I encourage complete openness and what comes up in the reading that day is meant to come up. While reading a clients cards, it is very important to take into account the feelings of the client, it is important to word things sensitively, especially if there is bad news to tell. Clients seem to believe the negative more quickly and ponder on the negative more readily than anything positive. So while reading cards, I would say please take this into account. I also believe, your cards are your choices, all that happens is your choice, apart from death, and even then that too can also be your choice. It is so important to leave the choice with the client, do not make preferences or any indications which you may feel is better. For example, if you are reading a lady's cards and you tell her that she will marry a tall dark handsome man, that lady will go out to dances, and no blonde, grey or red haired man would even have a chance. Always remember, nothing is written in stone because not only has the client got his/her choices but so do the people in the cards. Their choices also affect the clients life and decisions. The way I read the cards, the cards only go so far in your life and stop. When things start to happen, it means they have shifted out of the cards and it makes room for more information to come in. If there is more than one client, try to have more than one deck, as it takes a lot of shuffling from each client to get the last clients energy out of the cards and if it's not out in time, sometimes there can be traits in the next reading belonging to the last person. The cards should be read in a friendly way, if they can help people in the future that's all that matters.

There is a very old saying, that what falls on your floor, will come in your door. So if you the reader let a card fall, or the client, be sure to remember this, as you will find it actually is true.

Long ago, when people used ordinary cards for poker, which was also known in them days as the "devils game", there was a lot of stigma's attached because of this. Back in them days it was known to be unlucky to play cards from one day into the next, so the players would leave the cards down before midnight and lift them after midnight. The same goes for reading ordinary cards. I close my cards at five minutes before midnight and lift them five minutes after midnight. To close your deck all you do is look for the Ace of spades and the Ace of hearts, and face them together, then split the rest of the deck in half and put one half behind the Ace of spades and the other half behind the Ace of hearts so that the top and bottom of the deck have the outside pattern of cards showing. This protects you and your cards from any negativity.

When you feel you have worn out a deck of cards, just bin them. You should never use a deck for playing games when you use them for reading. When it comes to trying to read your won cards, I would discourage it very much. I know it is so tempting, but it can be addictive. I once compared giving up reading my own cards to giving up cigarettes. If you really need to know something, do it maybe once a week, but don't slip into a daily routine of it, it can mentally exhaust you.

Needless to say, because you read cards and in the line of work of helping people sort their lives out, you will find that a lot of people will pull out of you for help and energy. You will have to be strict with them for your own sake and health. It is also important to note that a reader should never read cards for nothing. The reader is not only reading cards but also giving the client a lot of energy, and that energy needs to be returned, other wise eventually the reader will burn out, and negative feelings and happenings occur to make the reader appreciate himself/herself. Even if it's a cup of tea from a sister or dinner from your mother, there has to be an exchange.

A question that is often asked is how often can your cards be read. I tell all my clients that the cards can be read as often as you like. Needless to say its better left till things have occurred which were predicted before. The more often you do the cards on the same day, the more likelihood of the cards picking up on the fears of the client.

As was said earlier, the client controls the cards completely. If there is something the client really deep down wants to hide, the cards will not show. Ina case like this, if the reader feels this is happening unknown to the client, the client should be told and if the situation does not change then the reader should talk to the client to keep the client occupied while shuffling, and then, out of the blue, take the cards from the client. Very often they will show an indication then of what's hidden because the client hadn't the chance to close the cards. I always say that when it comes to Weddings, Births and Deaths it is impossible to read them as these such events actually swamp the cards.

If a client comes to a reader wanting to know about a particular situation and on that day it doesn't show up in the cards, the client should be told that what they wanted to know today would've been in their cards had they had them read weeks, months ago. Cards do not always show what is happening today, very often it is in days, weeks or months ahead.

It is also important to note that complete confidentiality is required in card reading, no matter what the situation is, it is important that a client can feel at ease and confident that what is in their cards is between the reader and the client only. This is in the best interest of the reader as their reputation will be at stake.

Meanings of the cards

HEARTS ♥

The hearts relate to emotions, love, romance and feelings. In the tarot deck the hearts are represented by the cups.

Ace ♥

The Ace of Hearts is a powerful card, equally as powerful as all the Aces. When it is next to the Ace of Spades in a reading, it means someone's home, where they live. It is also used in the closing of the deck as explained earlier. When it comes up beside a picture card it can mean that a person is coming to the home. If with another of the aces it can indicate very important good changes.

2 ♥

The Two of Hearts is a strong love card in anyone's reading. It stands for a strong loving relationship. Beside the six of hearts it is a lover definitely returning from the past. It basically stands for someone returning into your company that used to be in it. Beside the two of diamonds, it means love and commitment, even marriage depending if the surrounding cards indicate it.

3 ♥

This is a beautiful card. It can mean a new beginning in someone's life, it can mean a baby especially if it lies between the king and queen. If it comes beside the seven of hearts it means someone is already pregnant. It can also mean a kiss. For example, if the three of hearts came beside the overseas cards, it could indicate anew start or life path overseas for the client.

4 ♥

This card indicates communication, basically by telephone. If this card falls on the floor you can be assured the phone will ring very shortly afterward. If it comes up beside the four of diamonds, it indicates two people moving in together or someone staying over in someone's house. If it falls beside the four of diamonds and the four of clubs it means that person will stay overnight in a hotel.

5 ♥

This is a very romantic card. It indicates someone speaking very romantically to the client. If, for example, the five of hearts falls in a reading beside the eight of diamonds it indicates a definite proposal of marriage. This is a card that every client would wish to have.

6 ♥

This card indicates a new romance, especially if it's with the two of spades because this implies a new romance with someone you do not know yet, a stranger. When it falls with the two of hearts it means a lover returning from the past but may try to change his / her ways from what you knew of him/her.

7 ♥

This card implies a growing love, for example, a child growing up. It can also mean a relationship getting stronger as time goes on. When lying beside the jack this is a definite child with the jack's features. If it falls beside a king or queen, it can mean a man or woman acting very childishly. The difference will be seen and felt by the cards around it. This is also a growing wish, something that you wish for will not be too far away.

8 ♥

This is the family card. If it falls beside a picture card, for example, the king of diamonds, this can mean a dad or granddad. If it falls beside the six of clubs it can mean a distant relative i.e. cousin.

9 ♥

This card is called the "Wish Card". When you do a client's cards for the first time, they should be told to make a wish and if the nine of hearts is in the bed, then their wish is not far away from them. If it lies beside a picture card, it can tell that the person whom it represents is very clever and intelligent and nice to have a conversation with. This person would be very much in the same line of thinking as the client.

10 ♥

This is called the "Love Conquers All" card. It is the strongest card in the deck. No matter what bad cards it falls beside you can be rest assured that all will be ok no matter what. When it falls with the nine of hearts it means the client is being looked after from above, heaven. It can also mean if it falls beside the king and queen that the couple are soul mates. It is very much a Divine Card. When it is situated with the ace of diamonds it can mean a wedding ring. When between the king and queen it means they can overcome any obstacle in their way.

JACK ♥

This is a picture card. It can represent a child or a person who is small in height or even an adult acting very childishly. The person can be of blonde, red or any light colouring. In some decks of cards this is a female card, in other decks it can be a male card. Either way, it is a very soft hearted person which really wouldn't do anyone any harm. This can also be someone in love, especially if there are romantic cards surrounding it.

QUEEN ♥

This is a lady of anything from blonde to light brown or red hair, blue or green eyes. She can be very soft hearted, sometimes too soft hearted, and as a result may leave herself very naïve regarding romantic matters. She wears her heart on her sleeve. She's always willing to give, doesn't matter if she doesn't get anything back. She yearns to be loved and is a very sensitive person as a result she can easily get hurt. When she does get annoyed with someone, she seems to forgive very quick, just can't hold a grudge for too long. This can also be someone of a darker colouring but actually they are in love. How you feel about the cards will show you which it is.

KING ♥

The king of hearts is a man with hair colouring from light brown, red to grey or even blonde. He may have blue, green or grey eyes. He has many of the characteristics of the queen of hearts but maybe not as naïve. He can also represent a darker featured man, but only if he's in love. This man isn't afraid to tell you about his ideas of his own life path and also isn't afraid of forecasting where he sees a relationship going if he's in love. At the same time he is very level headed when it comes to business. Like the queen, he is inclined to turn a blind eye to the people who do him wrong and give them too many chances; as a result he can sometimes be taken for granted. He is an honest and hard working person, in work as well as love.

DIAMONDS ♦

The understanding to this card is money, finances. The diamonds indicate business, wealth and power. The diamonds are equivalent to the coins/pentacles suit in the tarot deck.

ACE ♦

This indicates money, finances around a person. If surrounded with other diamonds you can be sure of any money difficulties disappearing. The ace of diamonds can also mean a ring or jewellery of some kind. When it comes beside the six of clubs you can be sure of a gift of jewellery unexpectedly. When the ace of diamonds comes beside the ace of hearts, depending on the surrounding cards, it can mean someone working from home.

2 ♦

This is a big money card especially when with the ten of diamonds. If the two of diamonds is between the two dark kings, the client or someone close is going into business or is already in business. If the two of diamonds fall between a king and queen, surrounded by hearts, this can be commitment in a loving relationship. If this two or any other falls beside the three of hearts it can mean the birth of twins, the reader will know by the nearby cards if this is so.

3 ♦

The three of diamonds can represent legal papers, documents, maybe even a will, especially if it is beside the king of diamonds. It can also mean a phone message when beside the four of hearts. It can also mean a key. If it lies beside the four of diamonds it means the keys to a house and if it lies with the four of clubs it means the keys of a car or other vehicle. It can also mean a cheque or money. The feeling you get and the surrounding cards will determine which it is.

4 ♦

This card represents a door, property. If this card falls out of the deck it indicates a new house for the person shuffling. If it falls beside the four of spades it means the client is definitely going to move house and if the seven of spades falls beside them, then the client will not be staying there either, the client will be moving again soon after.

5 ♦

The five of diamonds represents a job offer, or money being offered. If it falls beside the three, this can mean a new beginning in a job or a brand new job especially if the two of spades lies nearby. This can also help the reader find out what the client works at or will work at. If it falls beside the ace of spades, this can indicate a builder by trade. If it falls beside the four of diamonds it can indicate that the client is thinking of buying property. If the five of diamonds falls beside the six of diamonds it can mean a part-time job.

6 ♦

This is known as the poverty card. If this falls on the floor it indicates troubled times.

If the ten of diamonds is one side of a picture card and the six of diamonds is the other side of the picture card, this indicates that the person represented by the picture card has money, which is the ten of diamonds, but doesn't want to spend it, which is the six of diamonds. In other words, this person is a miser. This can also indicate that something is not good enough, for example, if it falls near the love cards it can tell that the client is not satisfied with the relationship. It can also indicate someone not doing their best in a situation.

7 ♦

This is the risk card. If this falls with the three of hearts, there is a chance that if the client is not careful there could be a pregnancy. In other words, the client has the choice. When the risk card comes up it means that the situation currently surrounding it has not happened yet and the outcome is up to the client. Another example is if it falls beside the six of diamonds the client risks a chance of becoming broke if they are spending unwisely.

8 ♦

This is the wedding card. If it falls with the five of hearts the client or someone very close will receive a marriage proposal. If it falls beside the five of diamonds there is a less romantic offer of marriage, perhaps a casual offer but meant sincerely. When the eight of diamonds comes beside the two of diamonds you can rest assured that this is the makings of a great marriage. If this card falls beside a picture card it means the person represented by the picture card is married. But if the nine of spades falls beside these two cards it means the person has a broken marriage. This can also mean great finances when surrounded by other diamonds.

9 ♦

One of the meanings of this card is a great job, permanent full time position. Beside a picture card it can mean that this person works very hard at their job. This card can also indicate an accident. For example, if it comes beside the four of clubs and the three of diamonds it can mean a car accident, the cards around it will show the reader whether it is very bad or minor. If it falls beside the home it can mean some one is getting work done at the home. When the nine of diamonds falls beside the seven of diamonds it can mean medication or drugs of some sort. When the nine falls beside the three of diamonds it can mean medical tests for the client or someone close. It can also be taken as someone having an operation.

10 ♦

This is the big money card. When it comes up with other diamonds the client can be assured money problems are on the way out. If it falls beside the business cards it means that business will go great. If it falls beside the three of diamonds and the king of diamonds it can indicate a substantial settlement of money in a legal case. When it comes up with a lot of diamonds around sometimes you can tell the amount that is coming. For example, the ten of diamonds can indicate one thousand or one hundred thousand depending on the severity of the situation. If the two of diamonds is beside it, it can sometimes indicate twelve or one hundred and twenty thousand. The feeling for the cards is important here.

JACK ♦

The jack of diamonds indicates a younger person of very light colouring, blonde, red or light brown. It can also represent a grown man acting very childishly. When it comes up beside the three of hearts and the seven of hearts it can indicate the sex of a baby unborn but it is wise not to go there as sometimes the cards can pick up the clients wants and hopes. Whether it is a man or a woman acting childishly or actually teenagers, it simply tells that this person is very insecure in themselves. Again in some decks the jack can be either male or female depending on what deck you have. The personality of the jack of diamonds is that of a clever and wise person, maybe a bit sharp with words when on the defensive.

QUEEN ♦

The queen of diamonds represents a blonde straight haired lady. It can also represent an older woman like someone's mother or also a woman who is financially well off. She is very sharp with her words, very cunning and sometimes suits herself more than others. She is very realistic and business minded, quickly on the mark. A very assertive lady who knows what she wants. The queen of diamonds is very much an authority figure.

KING ♦

The king of diamonds has many meanings. As indicated before he can represent a solicitor when surrounded by relevant cards. The king is a fair, red or grey haired man. He can also represent a father figure or grandfather. He is a man with a lot of years of wisdom. He can also be a husband or a very successful business man. This man is very knowledgeable and knows what he wants and how to get it. He is easy to get on with but it takes a lot of time to get to know him. He is a very loyal and faithful man to his family and friends. This man needs to learn more patience.

CLUBS ♣

The clubs are a very friendly suit. My own belief is that they represent growth and happiness and enthusiasm. They are very honest cards. The equivalent in the tarot is the wands.

ACE ♣

The ace of clubs is just as important as the other aces in the deck. It can represent papers, paperwork of some sort depending on the surrounding cards. If the ace falls upside down it can mean a delay or it can mean that the client will have to wait longer for the outcome to happen. When it comes up with any of the other aces it can mean new beginnings are very close. When the ace comes up beside a picture card I feel it can also mean that this person is on their own, maybe even lonely, depending on the surrounding cards.

TWO ♣

This is the friendship card. When it falls beside a picture card it tells you of the nature and character of a friend. If it comes with the five of clubs it can mean a friendly conversation.

THREE ♣

This card also represents paperwork. If it falls beside the king of diamonds it can mean a solicitors letter. It also represents an invitation of some sort. When it comes up beside the four of clubs it can be taken as an invite out for a night. When it falls beside diamond cards it can mean a letter which also contains money. Not very often have I seen it, but if it comes up beside the six of clubs it can mean that the client actually possess the same gift of reading cards. When it comes up with the nine of clubs or nine of diamonds it can also mean legal papers. The three can also mean time i.e. 3 weeks, months but never years.

FOUR ♣

This card represents a place of entertainment i.e. hotel, pub etc., places where a lot of people congregate. When the four of clubs falls with the three of diamonds it represents a car or vehicle. When it comes up with the ten of clubs it can mean some one is drunk, it can also mean someone driving long distance if it comes beside the car, depending on the cards surrounding it. If it falls with two fives of any suit it can mean someone speeding or going somewhere in too much of a hurry. If the four of clubs falls beside the ace of hearts it can mean a mobile home. If it comes up with the eight of hearts it can mean a family get together. Beside the ace of diamonds it means someone's getting a date.

FIVE ♣

This card represents someone asking questions and getting no answers. It is a communication card. Beside the four of clubs it means someone is getting asked out. Beside the diamonds, someone is asking for money.

SIX ♣

This card has a few meanings. The first one is a gift. If it falls with i.e. ace of diamonds it means someone will receive a gift of a ring or jewellery of some sort. If it is beside the five of clubs the person has the gift of the gab, knows what to say and when to say it. This card can also mean distance. If it falls beside the four of diamonds it can mean the client is keeping his distance from that house. If it falls beside the five of diamonds it can mean a job offer but a lot of travelling to and from. Also if it falls beside the eight of hearts it can mean a distant relative, like a cousin.

SEVEN ♣

This card represents victory, success. If a situation comes up and this card appears you can rest assured it will turn out for the best.

EIGHT ♣

This is the luckiest card in the deck. If it comes up with the three of diamonds you could have a winning ticket. I also feel this is a fate card, for example, if the client is having a rough patch in life and this comes up, I always say that it's all happening for a reason, there's something the person has to learn or see in the situation they're in. This is also an affectionate card. When it comes up with the seven of hearts beside a king and queen it means a couple are being very intimate in a loving way. If it comes up with the three of diamonds it can mean contraception, i.e. the pill. If it comes up with the three of clubs it can mean condoms. If it comes up with the ace of spades it can mean sexy clothes. In some cases, it can mean a weekend away especially if it comes up with the four of clubs.

NINE ♣

This is also a wish card. Again when it is beside the three of clubs it can mean legal papers. When it falls beside a jack of spades it can mean definite legal papers but the prospect of court. The jack and nine of clubs together can illustrate a barrister.

TEN ♣

This card represents communication. If it falls beside the three of clubs it can mean someone studying for exams. There is a lot of chat when this is about. It can also mean distance when it comes beside the three of diamonds and the four of clubs. This ten can also mean time, in the space of ten weeks, months.

JACK ♣

The jack of clubs represents a young girl with hair colouring of brown to dark brown with a curl in it. She is very jolly in nature and full of chat. She can be very naive and innocent. This can also represent a young woman who is maybe small in height and quite childish. She is very honest and hard working and sincere, a very good friend to have.

QUEEN ♣

The old meaning of this card is the no sex card. It can mean no intimacy in a relationship. This lady is of brown to dark brown. She is very cunning and in touch with what's going on around her. Very intuitive person, very trustworthy, would take a secret to her grave. She can be a bit over powering sometimes and only considers her own feelings until it's pointed out to her. She can be very critical of men, an old fashioned person in a lot of ways but she would need not to be crossed. She loves being the centre of attention but unfortunately her mood swings tend to frighten people away and as a result she may have traits of a "poor me".

KING ♣

This is a man of brown to dark brown, even grey colouring. This man knows more than what he lets on he does. In a lot of ways he is very much a person who suits himself and doesn't take into account other people's feelings. This man can enjoy time on his own but in relationships, he can be sometimes a fly by night character. This man wants a relationship that suits him. With the right person he can be loving, understanding and very gentle.

SPADES ♠

The spades were always associated with evilness or bad luck of some sort but in the contrary the spades are actually a friendly suit. There is no negativity in my cards when they are read. The worst is death and unfortunately it is something we are all sure of happening and can't avoid at some stage. The way I read cards, this suit has so many meanings that you can not depict one meaning for a spade. The equivalent of this suit in the tarot is the swords.

ACE ♠

The ace is just as powerful as the rest of the aces. Unfortunately this ace has a bad reputation but as you will see, it's not all that bad at all. It can represent a building or a city depending on what's surrounding it. When it's beside the five of diamonds it can be took as a builder or someone getting work done to premises. When it falls upside down it can represent a uniform especially if it falls beside the nine's in the deck. This can indicate an emergency uniform i.e. Gardi or nurses etc. It can also just mean clothes when not with the nine's.

TWO ♠

This card represents uncertainty. It shows that someone is not sure of something. If it falls beside the six of hearts for example, it can be taken as a new romance with someone the client hasn't met yet, someone the client doesn't know already. When this comes up in a reading I would always advise the client to stand back from the situation and in time, the right way will come about.

THREE ♠

This card depicts disloyalty. If it comes up in a romantic spread, all is not being revealed. It can indicate that there is a third party involved in a relationship. If it falls with the two of spades beware as the disloyalty will surely reveal itself in time. The three and two together can also mean behind back bighting, someone talking nice to your face and talking bad of you behind your back. When it appears in a spread beside the seven of diamonds I always inform the client to only tell people what you feel they should know, nothing more because if you do, it will come back to you with legs and arms.

FOUR ♠

This indicates that a door is closed. Let it be an actual door to a house or door to emotions. It can indicate the person that has moved is not in or not wiling to communicate. The difference will be known in the spread. If it falls beside the four of diamonds it is surely a change of address. If it falls beside the five of diamonds it can mean the sale of property. If it falls beside the nine of diamonds it can mean someone leaving their job. If the four of hearts and the four of diamonds come up beside the job card it can indicate a move either in the present job or a new job in a new area.

FIVE ♠

This represents troubles and strife. This is not a bad card, it just tells of tough times coming and to be patient, it will pass. It can also indicate a lot of worry unnecessarily. It also represents fear. If it falls beside a picture card and the two of diamonds it can mean that the person is afraid of commitment in a relationship. Sometimes it can be very much self inflicted by the client. If it comes up beside the four of clubs and the three of diamonds it can mean there's something wrong with a car, but if the ten of clubs is there also it can mean someone is afraid of driving.

SIX ♠

This card indicates travel. It can mean across the border into another country. For example, if it falls beside a picture card it means that the person is from across the border or has a northern accent. If it falls with the five of diamonds it can indicate the offer of work across the border. It just indicates something/someone not from this country, from a nearby country.

SEVEN ♠

This indicates something is not over. This is the card that every couple who has problems wants to see in a reading. If a client has fallen out with a partner or friend and this card falls, then it is surely not over no matter how hard that is to see. This represents continuation. If this comes up with troublesome cards you know that the client has had these problems before, they are reoccurring until they are dealt with.

EIGHT ♠

This card represents depression, sickness. If it falls beside the nine of diamonds and the seven of diamonds you can be sure the client or someone close is on medication for depression. Depending on the cards around it if it falls beside the seven of spades it can mean cancer reoccurring. The difference will be surly be seen and felt in nearby cards. If it falls beside the four of spades it can mean the sickness is coming to an end. When it falls also beside the eight of clubs it tells of disappointing news. The eight can also mean a journey that someone doesn't really want to take. This sometimes comes up after a person has had an operation and when the good cards come down upon it you know all will be well.

NINE ♠

This card means "The parting of the ways". It indicates a break in communication between people. If it falls beside the marriage card it tells of a marriage break-up. This card indicates big changes not only physically but also mentally. If the four of spades comes with it, there is no going back to communications with the person. If it falls with the ten of hearts, love conquers all, it indicates a death. If there's a picture card near both cards it can indicate who it relates to. If there are other dark cards about, the eight of spades or five of spades, it would appear that the death is physical. If not it can mean the death of a relationship or friendship. If the nine of spades and the ten of hearts falls beside the two of clubs do not take it that your friend will die, it can mean the end of the friendship and it could also be someone else, a friend that the client might here of. If it falls beside the family card it doesn't mean someone in the client's family will die, it can indicate someone close to him/her, their family. I state this now as it is so very important not to say this to clients unless you can be sure. Please take care when approaching this subject with clients.

TEN ♠

This card indicates travelling overseas, especially if it falls with the six of spades. If it's work related the relevant cards will also be there but if it's a holiday the four of clubs should be somewhere close. If it falls with the ten of clubs also it can be taken as a trip overseas. If it comes up with the five of diamonds and four of diamonds it can indicate someone buying property overseas. It also can be taken as an argument. If it comes down with the five of spades between picture cards, the client should be warned of an argument in which she/he could be involved. If it falls with the nine of spades it can mean a violent argument leading to someone getting hurt.

JACK ♠

The jack of spades is a young, very dark haired, maybe dark skinned person. He can represent a grown man but with child like character. Very cunning man. He is light hearted and friendly and would say more than his prayers. Very hard to find out what this person actually

44

thinks. He doesn't like thinking or even talking long-term, he's a person who lives for the day. Sometimes can be very irresponsible and needs a lot of growing up. Being with this person will not be easy, very up and down relationship. This can also indicate a guy who is small in height. When the jack falls with the nine of clubs it represents a barrister in a court case.

QUEEN ♠

The queen of spades is a very dark haired lady with a lot of hidden qualities. It can also be a fairer haired lady with a bad temper, depending on nearby cards. She is very kind and loyal to her friends and would help them in anyway she could. When she is angry there is no talking to her, she would need to be on her own to let her temper settle. She is the most intuitive of all the suits. She likes to be mysterious and intriguing to men to keep their interest in her.

KING ♠

The king of spades is a very dark haired man, can be going grey. A very clever and educated man who knows what he wants and wont settle for anything less. A very stubborn man if he can't get what he wants. He is very honest, loyal and down to earth. The king tends to see everything in black and white, there's no room for grey. It's either right or wrong. He would find it hard to show how he feels with a woman, he would feel he would have to drop his pride. Things are either his way or no way. This can also be a lighter haired man in a very bad temper, the difference would be seen in the surrounding cards.

Relevant additions to a reader

When all the four aces come together, touching each other, this clearly means that something completely unexpected is about to occur. This something will definitely bring about changes that could never have been even dreamt. Whether the outcome is good or not so good depends on the surrounding cards.

When the four two's come together this means shocking news is going to be heard. If only three two's come together then there is an alarm of some sort coming.

When the four three's come together this can be someone planning something behind backs. Whether good or not so good depends on surrounding cards.

When the fours all come together it indicates good opportunities coming. When three four's are together the client needs to relax a bit more, he/she maybe over doing things.

When the four five's come together it tells of great speed, someone maybe going too fast in a situation and needs to step back. When three five's are together it means decisions need to be made but at ease.

When the four six's come together it tells of things not happening as quick as the client would like. When the three six's are together it means that an opportunity is offered that would need to be looked into, it may not be all it seems.

When the four seven's come together it indicates talk of children i.e. starting up a family. When the three seven's are together it represents definite success in a situation.

When the four eight's come together it can indicate a proposal of marriage. When the three eight's come together it shows disappointments.

When the four nine's come together this represents a robbery either to do with the client or someone close to them. When the three nine's come together it represents an emergency of some sort i.e. Doctor, police, hospital etc.

When the four ten's come together it represents big changes in direction of life here or abroad. When the three of ten's come together it can represent financial gain.

When the four jacks come together it indicates deceit from someone close. When the three jacks are together it shows disputes.

When the four queens come together it shows scandalous gossip which is not good at all. When the three queens come up it represents ladies just having a friendly chat, swapping opinions.

When four kings come together it also shows men talking and the client is topic of conversation. When the three kings come together it tells of a conference, maybe a business meeting.

It is important to note that any man or woman can change their suit in the cards at any time. Because they find their picture card that represents them it doesn't mean that this is the only card to show them. Life changes and so do people so therefore their suits change too.

Each person is entitled to take from the meanings what suits them and leave out what doesn't. If the reader has the feeling for the cards they will know what meanings agree and what don't.

Before doing a reading I personally always ask for Devine Guidance, call in your angles, Holy Spirit, past relatives, anyone you feel comfortable with. Ask for help in seeing and feeling what's in the cards and to help you give each client a good reading. Even light a candle where the reading is taking place.

Methods of reading

Reading another person's cards is a chance to see into another person's life. It is therefore important that the client feels comfortable and confident in you as a reader. They need to know that their deepest secrets will always remain that way. The reader therefore needs to be very understanding, non judgemental, sensitive and honest. When a person comes to get their cards read it is because they need clarity in their life regarding some situation and the reader needs to know that it's only up to them to clarify and not to tell the client what to do, that it is his/her decision.

Intuition is very important because when the cards are vague it's the reader's feelings and intuition that makes the reading clear. It is the card reader's responsibility to remain as positive as possible throughout the reading as some clients hang on to every word. There are three methods of reading that I would use and I will go through each.

THE BED

The Bed, or Celtic Cross as some would call it is a very old method of reading. It represents what is happening right now in the client's life. The five cards below the bed go into the future. If something, which happened in the past, is affecting the client today and maybe stopping him/her from moving forward, this sometimes would come up in the cards that actually make the bed. As the client puts the cards down upon the bed and the five below cards, it tells how the situation will progress as each card goes down. I use the whole deck of cards, some readers would only use a few cards. When the bed is being started I ask the client to shuffle the cards for a while and when he/she feels they're ready, to go from the start of the deck to the end of the deck, randomly picking out seventeen cards. If they come to the end of the deck and they haven't enough, just go through the deck again until I tell them I have the seventeen I need. When I'm making the bed it is important for the client to hold the remaining cards without shuffling them, until I tell him/her to start putting them down. This makes sure the clients energy is still in the cards. When making the bed the cards are put into position with the cards facing down, in other words, the numbers not showing just the back of the cards.

FIG. 1

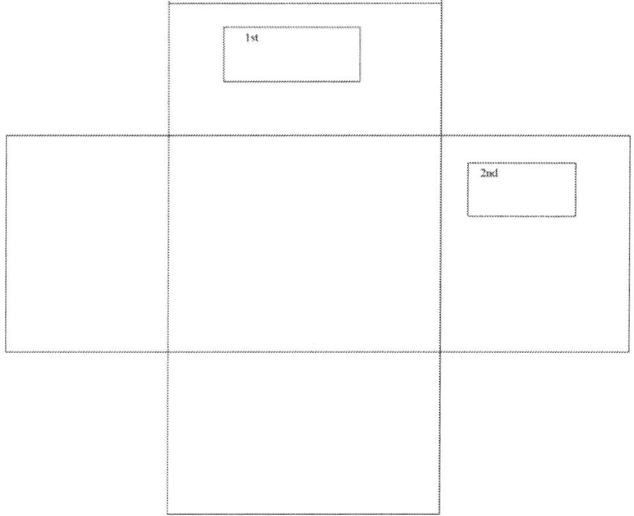

FIG. 2

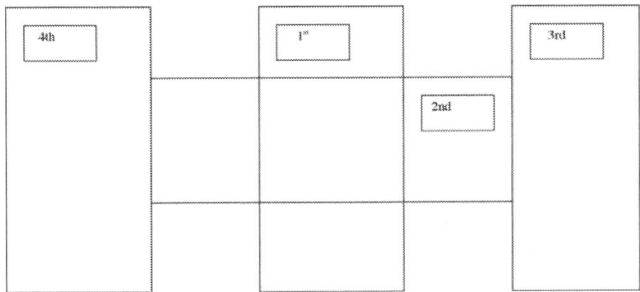

The second card lies across the first card. When you put the third card down on the right it sits on top of the end of the second card on the right. When you put the fourth card down on the left it sits on top of the end of the second card on the left.

FIG. 3

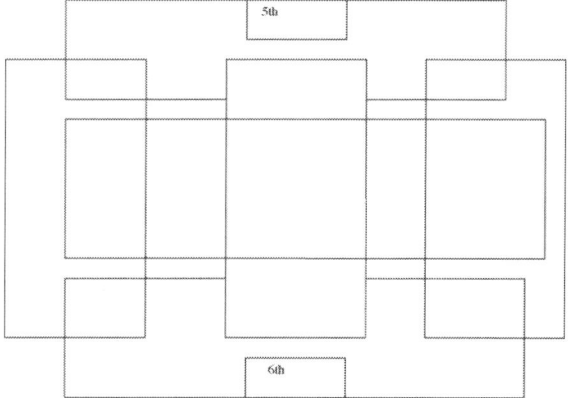

The fifth card is placed under the top of the first card and over the tops of the third and fourth. The sixth card is placed under the bottom of the first card and over the bottoms of the third and fourth. When this is done you push all cards together and they should hold together. They should look like Fig. 4.

FIG. 4

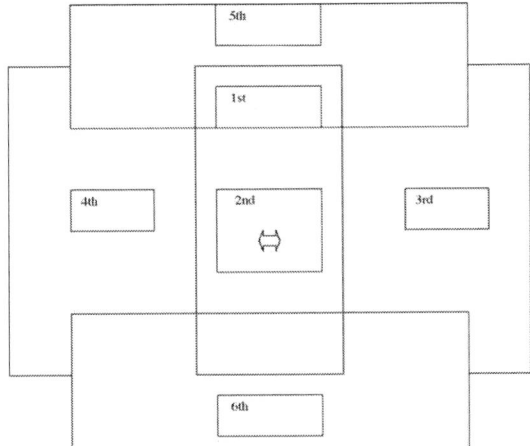

FIG. 5

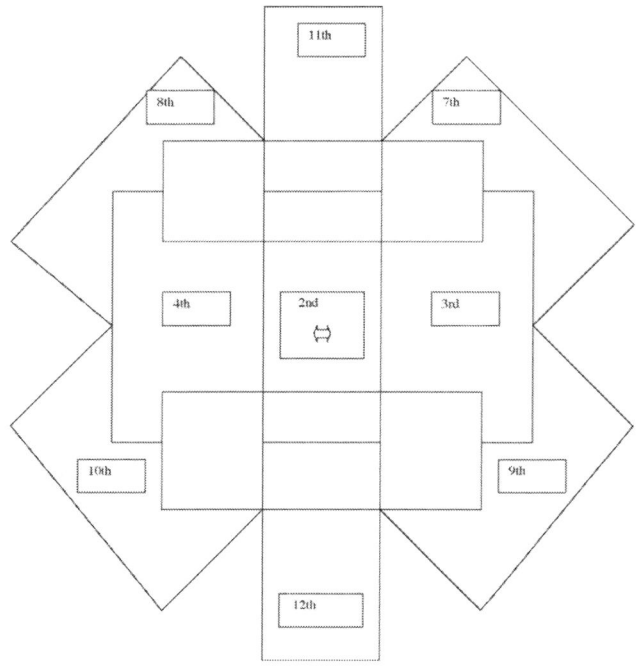

At this stage it looks more complicated than it is. The seventh card slots in behind the fifth and third card and is held in place by the right corner of the first card. The eight card slots in behind the fifth and fourth card and is held in place by the left corner of the first card. The ninth card is slotted in behind the third and sixth card and is held in position by the right bottom corner of the first card. The tenth card is slotted in behind the fourth and sixth card and is held in position by the bottom left corner of the first card. The eleventh card slots in behind the top of the first card and the twelfth card slots into the bottom of the first card.

Then the remaining five cards that are left are placed below the bed.

The bed and the five cards should look like Fig. 6

FIG. 6

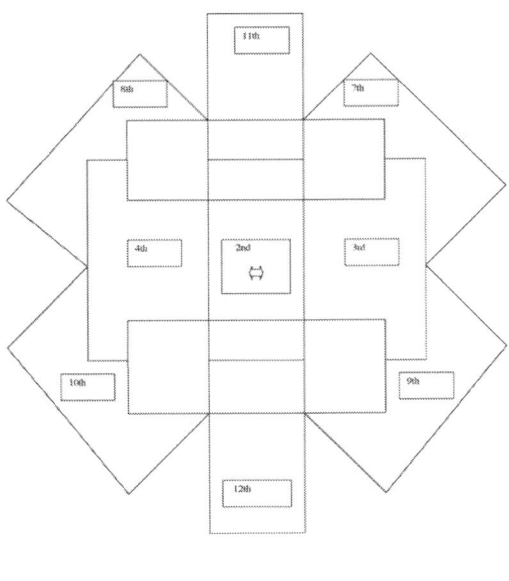

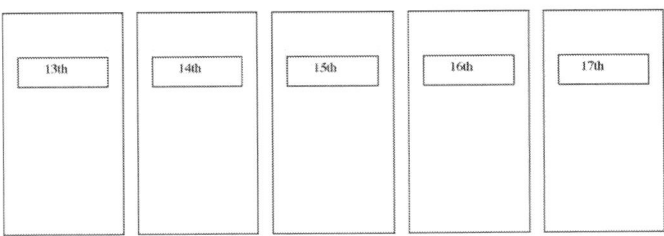

When the bed is made the reader turns it over to see the number side and when it's turned over, the client is told to make a wish. If the nine of hearts is in the bed the wish will surely come true. It's now that the reader needs to know the meanings of each card and also to listen to their gut instinct. If the two middle cards are a king and queen it can actually represent a man and woman in bed together very intimately. If the three of hearts is next to them it surely means sex resulting in pregnancy. Another example, if two picture cards are touching and heads of picture cards very close it can mean two people kissing. The story reveals itself as the client puts down each card at a time. The reader can tell the client to halt at any time during the reading so that the meanings and feelings can be depicted. The client should think carefully where he/she wants the cards to go, whether on top of bed or the five cards below the bed. As the reading progresses all the cards should be touching each other, whether they're on top of each other or even lying sideways on each other. The cards will only tell so far into the future and then they'll stop. When the predictions start to happen in the client's life, it means that these events have shifted out of the cards and there is more room in the cards again. Therefore the client will be able to get the cards read again. Always remember it is not written in stone.

LONG – TERM READING

The second type of reading cards is a lot more simpler. It would be more long-term and I usually do this for a client after the bed is done.

As usual, the cards need to be well shuffled and when the client feels this the deck is handed to the reader and the reader puts the cards down. The cards are put down with the number side facing the reader. They are put in a line of six cards across and four cards down, all touching each other. See Fig. 1 below.

FIG. 1

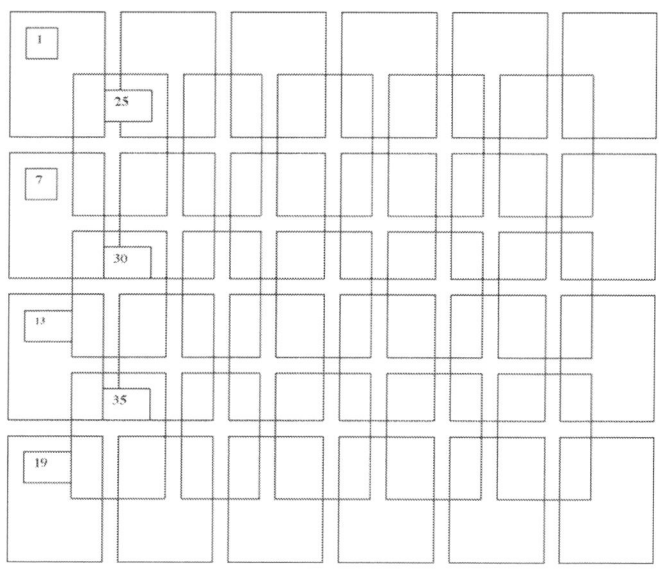

The twenty fifth card lies on top of the first, second and seventh and eight cards. To get a clear picture make sure that all the cards are touching each other. You carry on putting the cards down and now you have a row of five cards across and three down. You then put a row of four cards across with the first sitting on card twenty five and twenty six and thirty and thirty one and carry on until you have four across and two down. Then you put the three across and lastly the two last cards sit on top beside each other.

These cards can be read anyway, just see what cards lie beside each other taking into account the cards directly underneath.

When a reader does their own cards it's always better to do the long-term as the cards are put down one after the other, whereas in the bed the reader knows what cards are already down.

SIX WAYS TO A HAPPY FUTURE

The last method is called the six ways to a happy future. This can be used when a person is already in a relationship. It consists of a poem that ends with a kiss. The poem is as follows.

> One pile for me
> One pile for thee
> One for health
> One for wealth
> One for my friends
> (Add a kiss to blend)
> And a pile for love that never ends.

For this spread, the joker needs to be included in the deck. Choose the picture card that you feel represents you and your partner. Think of your partner and your relationship while giving the full deck of cards a good shuffle. Then when you feel you've shuffled enough, ask the cards whatever question you like while the deck is still in your hand. Then cut the deck in two with your left hand. Choose which pile you want to start with and keep both piles face down. Say the first line of the poem and when you reach the last word put face down the first card of the pile you have chosen out on top. Say the second line and put your second card next to the first one, repeat the next three lines and put each card adjacent to the other two. You don't deal a card for the sixth line. Then the seventh line, you kiss the card and put it adjacent to the rest. You now have six cards side by side. You then deal the rest of the pile you choose the same way, using the poem and putting the cards face down on top of the previous six cards. Do this until all the cards are dealt. Because you have fifty three cards, including the joker, there will be five cards left to deal when you say the poem for the last time.

When you say "add a kiss to blend" just kiss your hands and rest them on the sixth pile while saying the last words. Turn the first card over in each pile and see how it fits in with the line of the poem it represents. For love and romance the piles one, two and six are the most important. If you can't get enough information from the first card of each pile, turn over the next card below it in the pile.

If you find the picture cards that you picked out earlier that represent you and partner in the piles one, two and six, then this tells of a long lasting relationship. If neither is found then you could be doing a rethink of your situation. If only one picture card is found it means the relationship will need a lot of work.

The last word

You now know all there is to know about card reading, well all that I know and I too am still learning something new each day. You can practice as much as you like but always remember when doing your own cards that you can become addicted to them if you do them too much. It is always easier to do strangers then people close as you feel less pressure. Beware of befriending clients as you can find that they too can end up being too attached to you and the cards. It is also important to note that what ever comes out is not one hundred percent proof or accurate, people do make mistakes. Remind clients that their future lies in their own hands, you can offer advice, show them their choices but you cannot tell them which road is best, that is for them to choose. As a reader you too need to look after yourself, pamper yourself, treat yourself nicely after doing a clients cards, it can be a very draining experience at times. Reading cards really opens your eyes to life and how other people's lives are for them. You meet so many different people. Be prepared for negative criticisms and do not take them on board, always try to keep positive energy throughout the reading and afterwards.

I really hope you get as much out of card reading as I have.

Goodluck!

ISBN 141203371-3

9 781412 033718

Made in the USA
Lexington, KY
05 December 2010